Crazy Emoji & Emotion Monsters Awesome Coloring Book

By

Adriana P. Jenova

Anti-Stress Art Therapy adult coloring book

Volume 3

Published by PUBLISHING COMPANY in 2016
First edition: First printing
Illustrations and design © 2016 Adriana P. Jenova

allcoloringbook.com

ISBN-13: 978-1540673121
ISBN-10: 154067312X

LOVE
CHAT On line
SD
WTF
TTYL
ZZZ
IDK GR8 SRY
ALS K8 RY
JK KL
1OQ 8
LMFAO
LOL
BRB
TTYL
GM

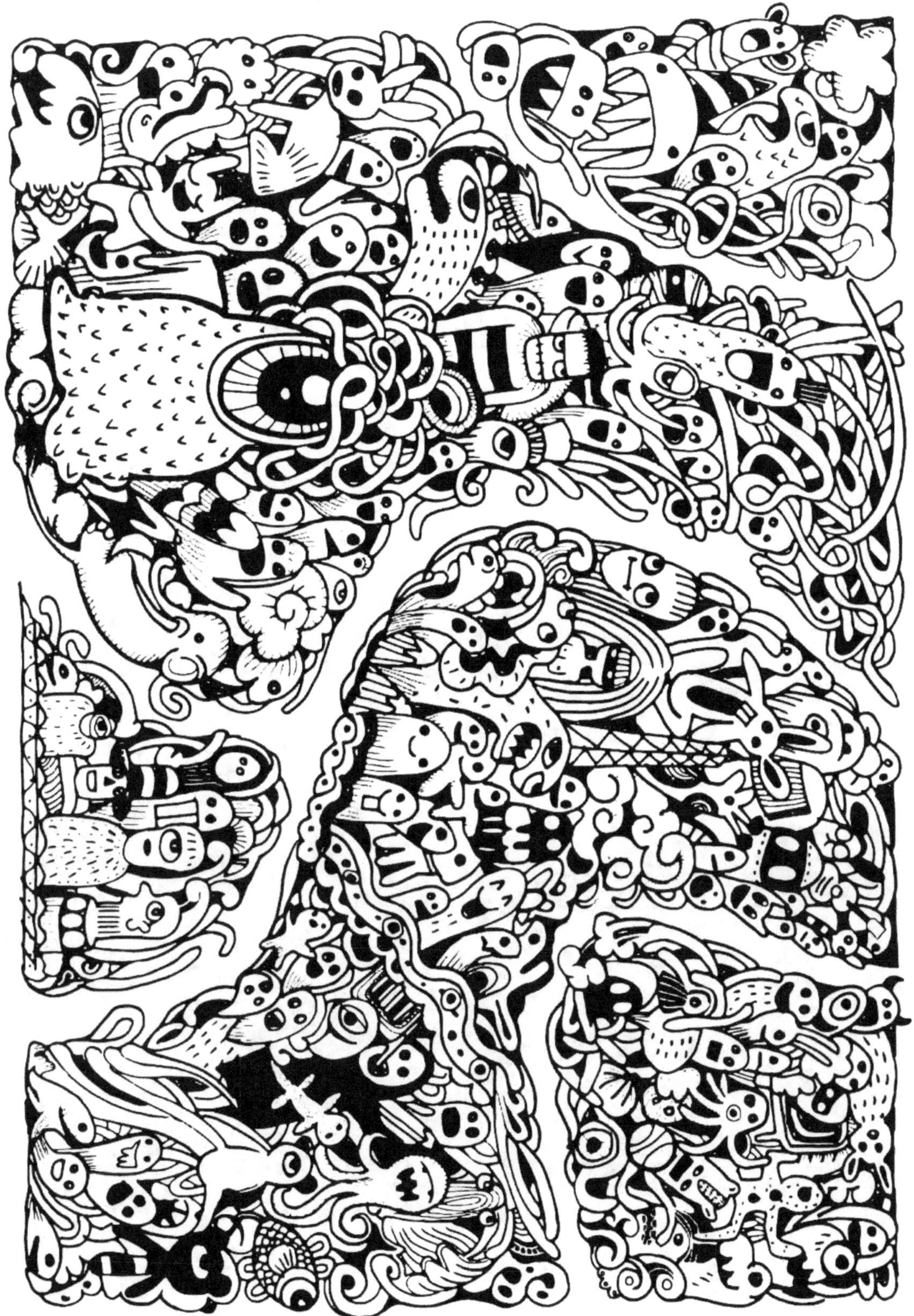

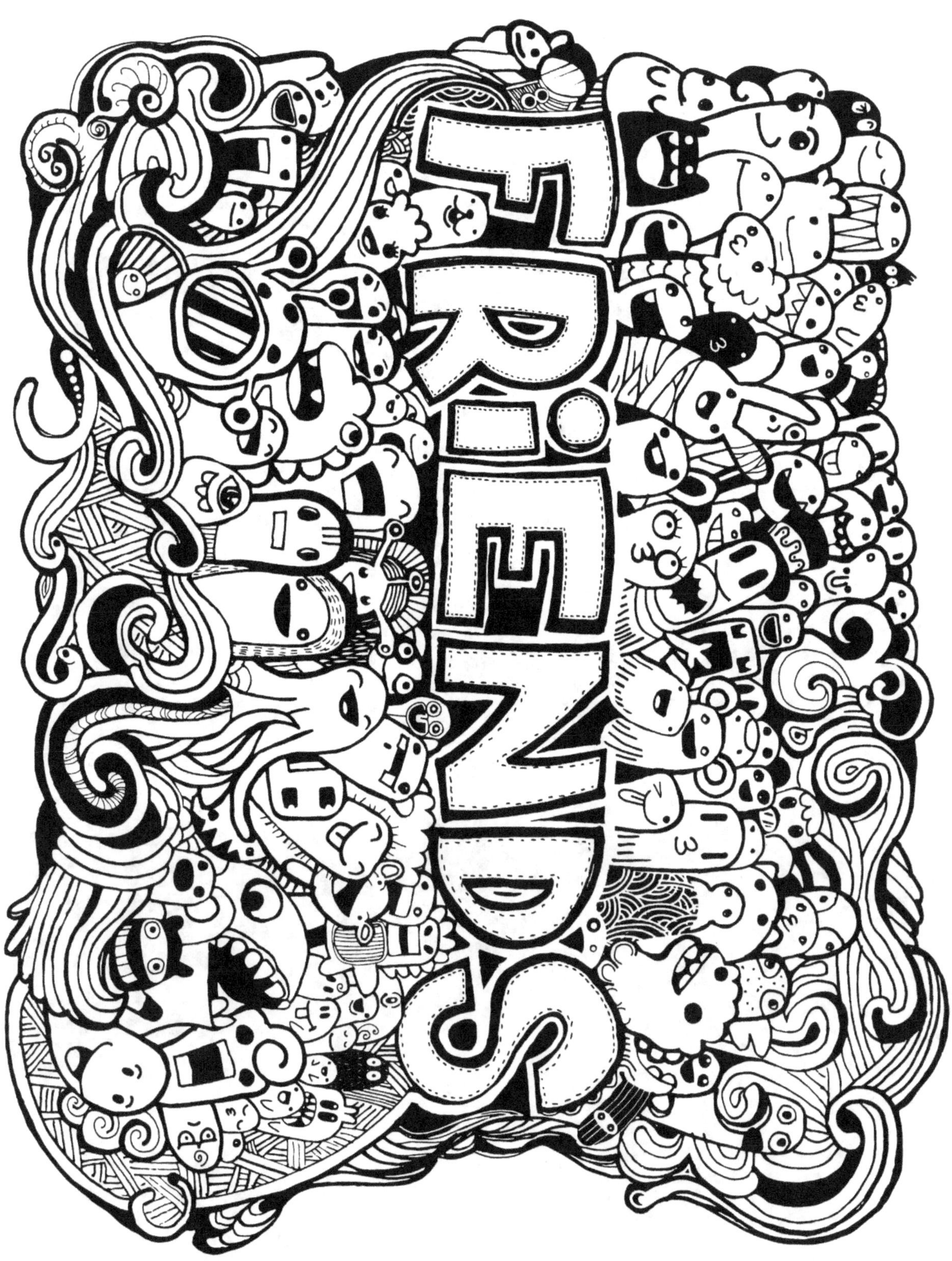

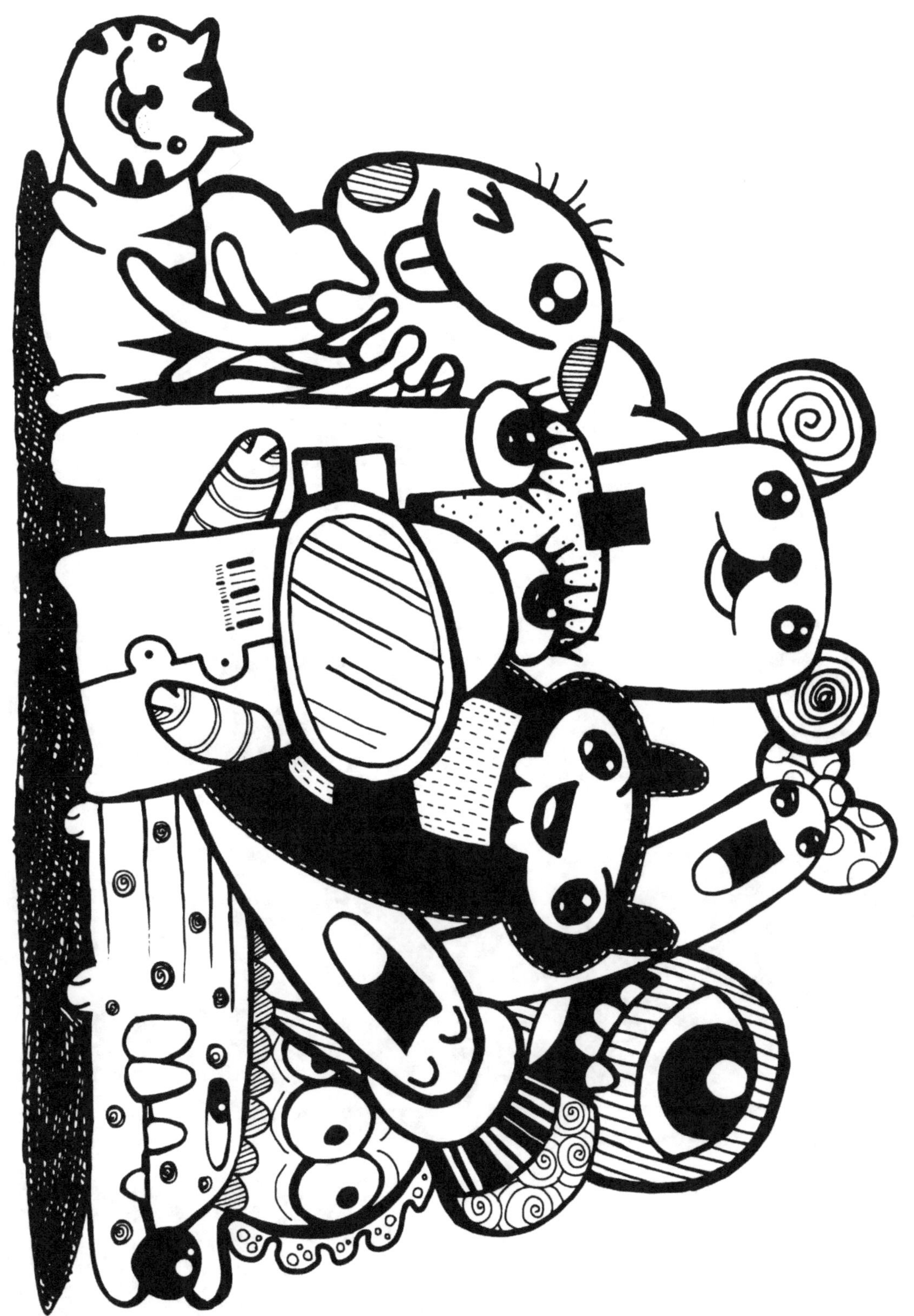

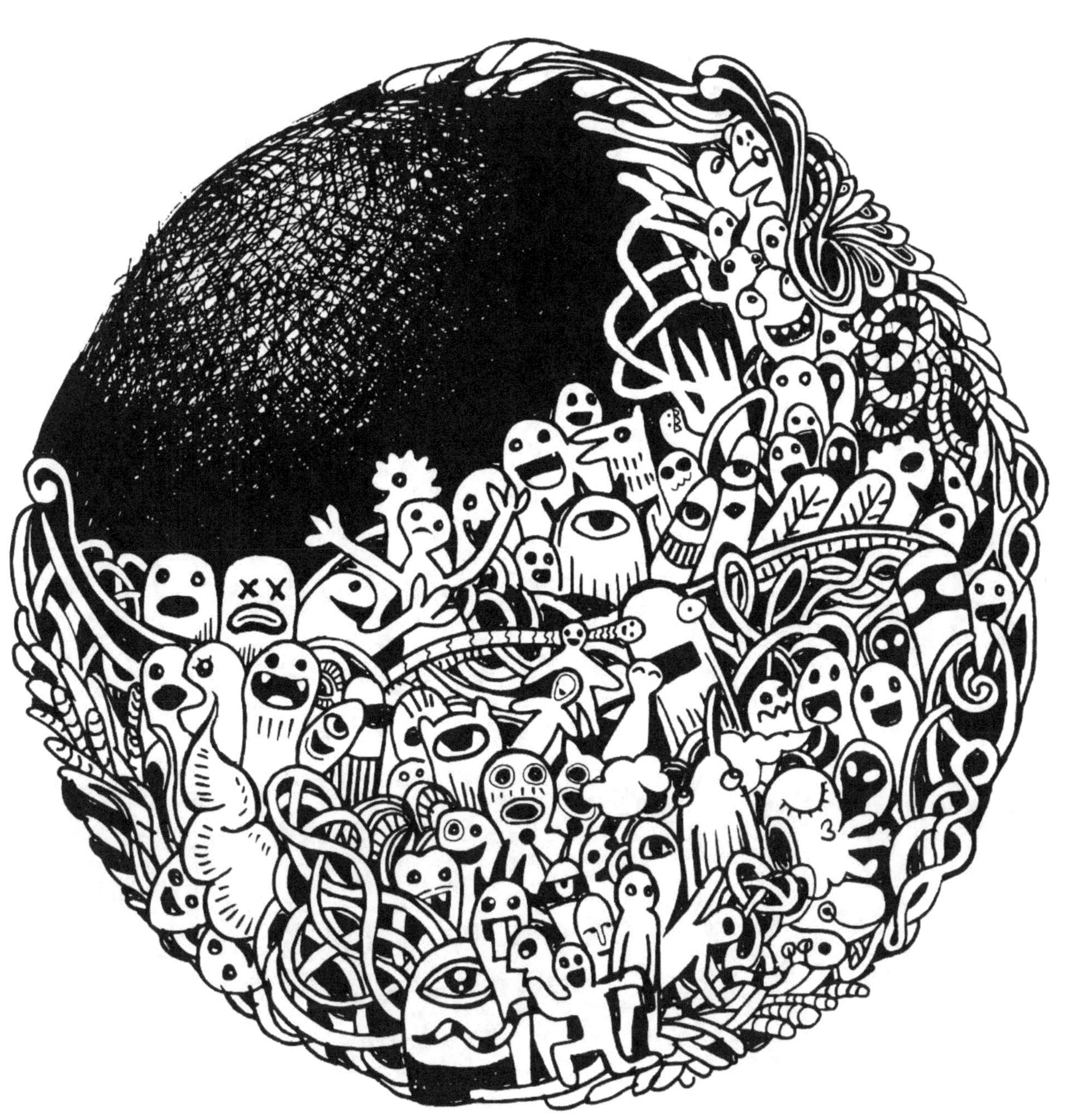

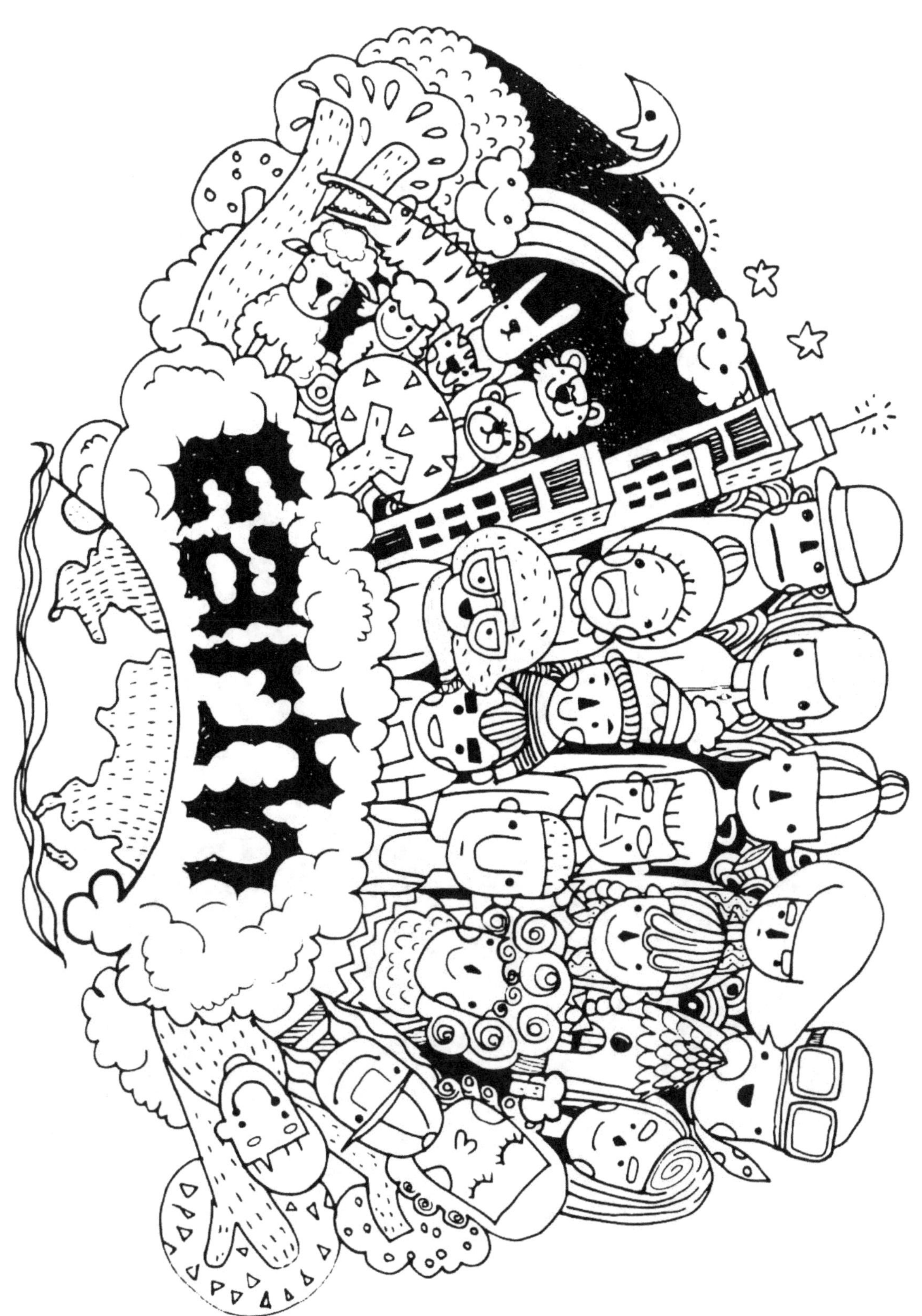

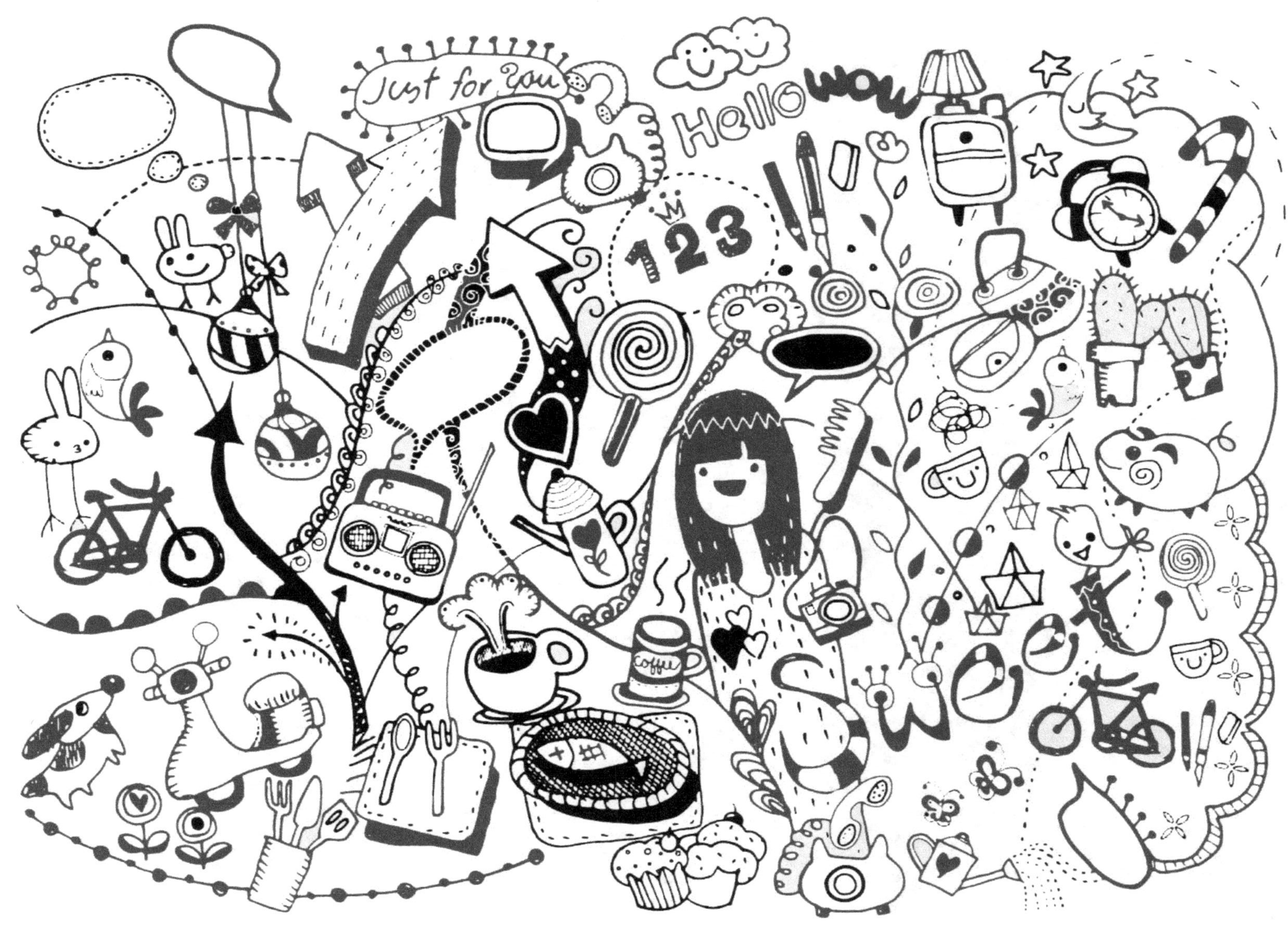

Just for you
Hello
wow
123
Coffee
Sweet

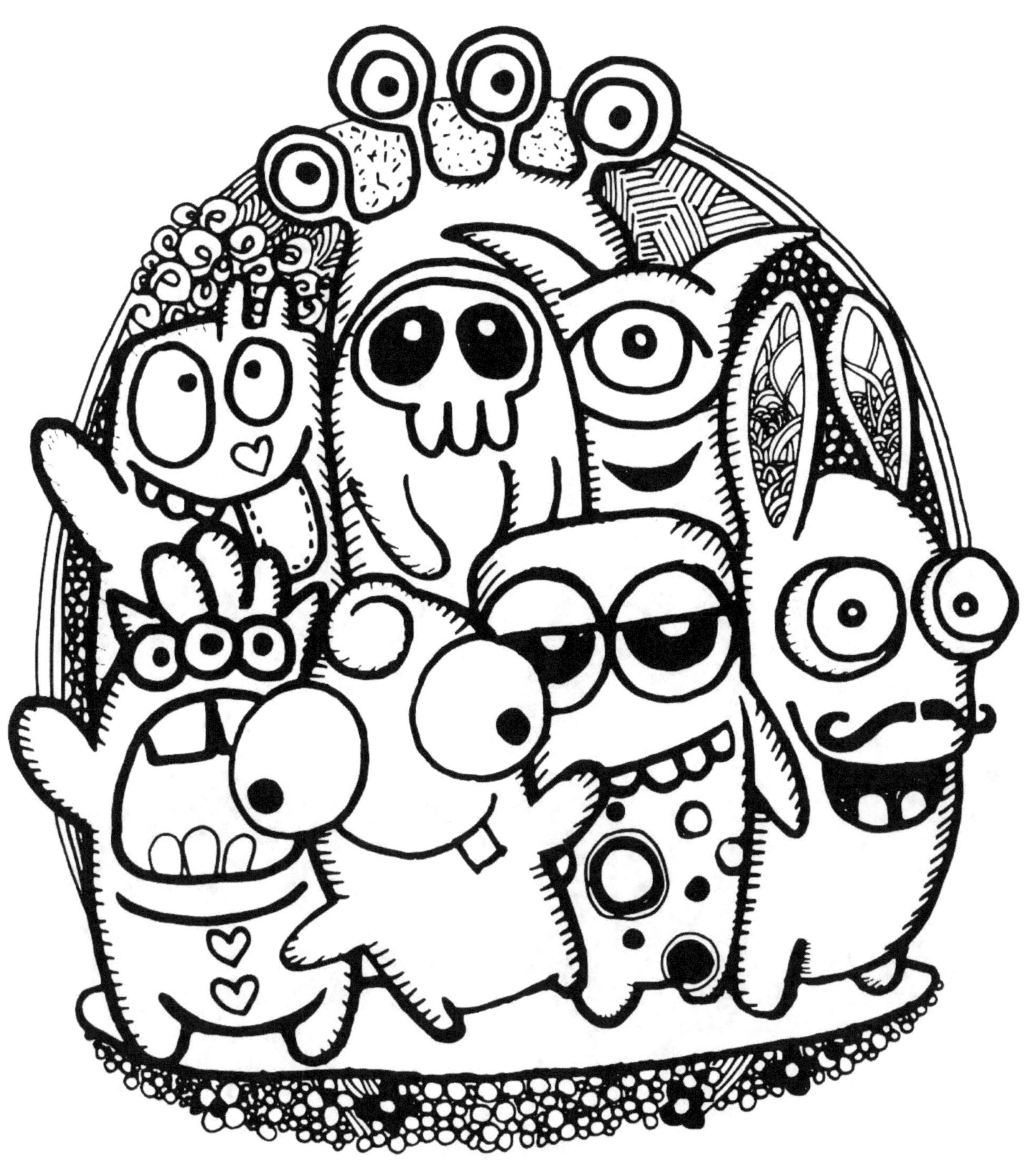

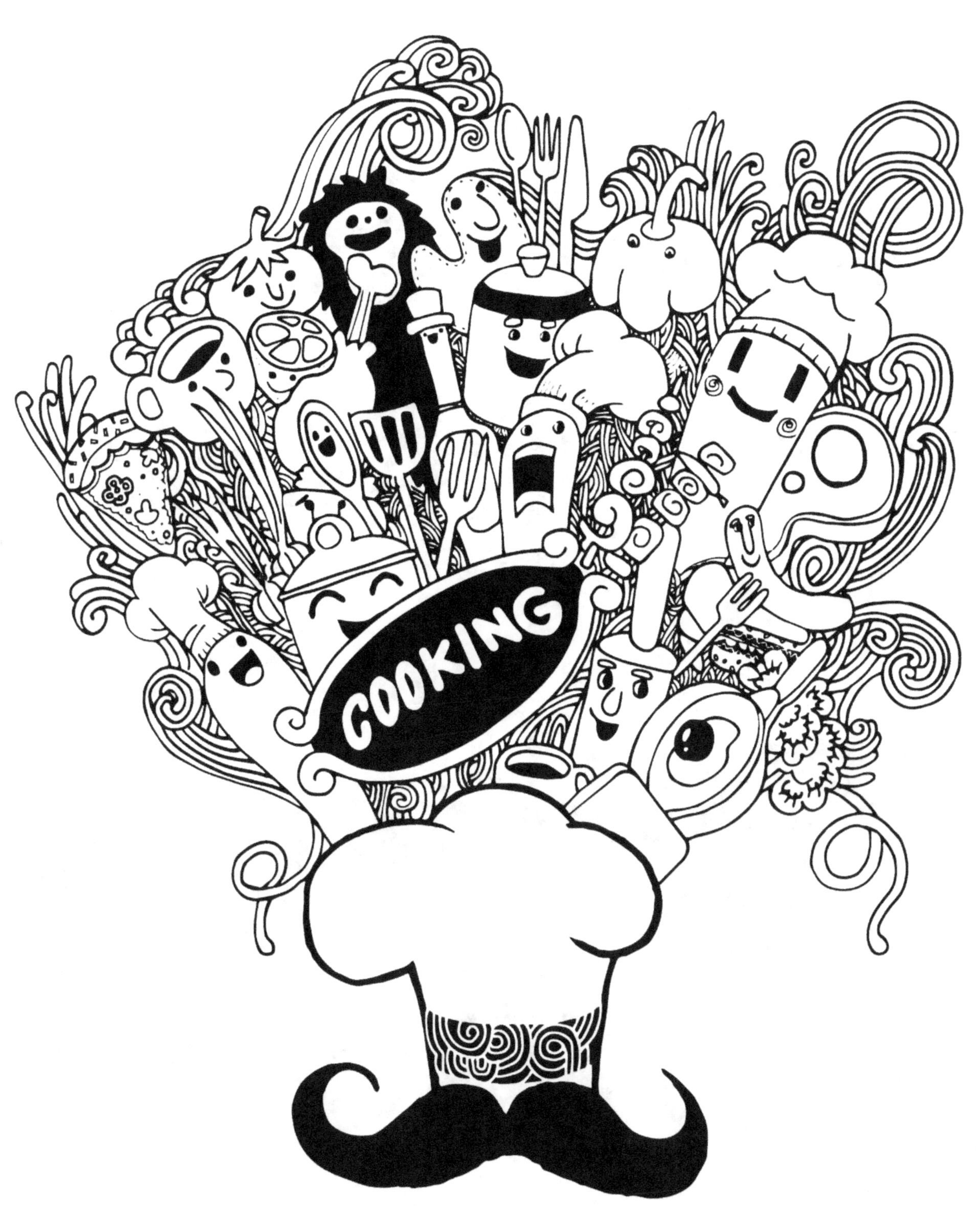
COOKING

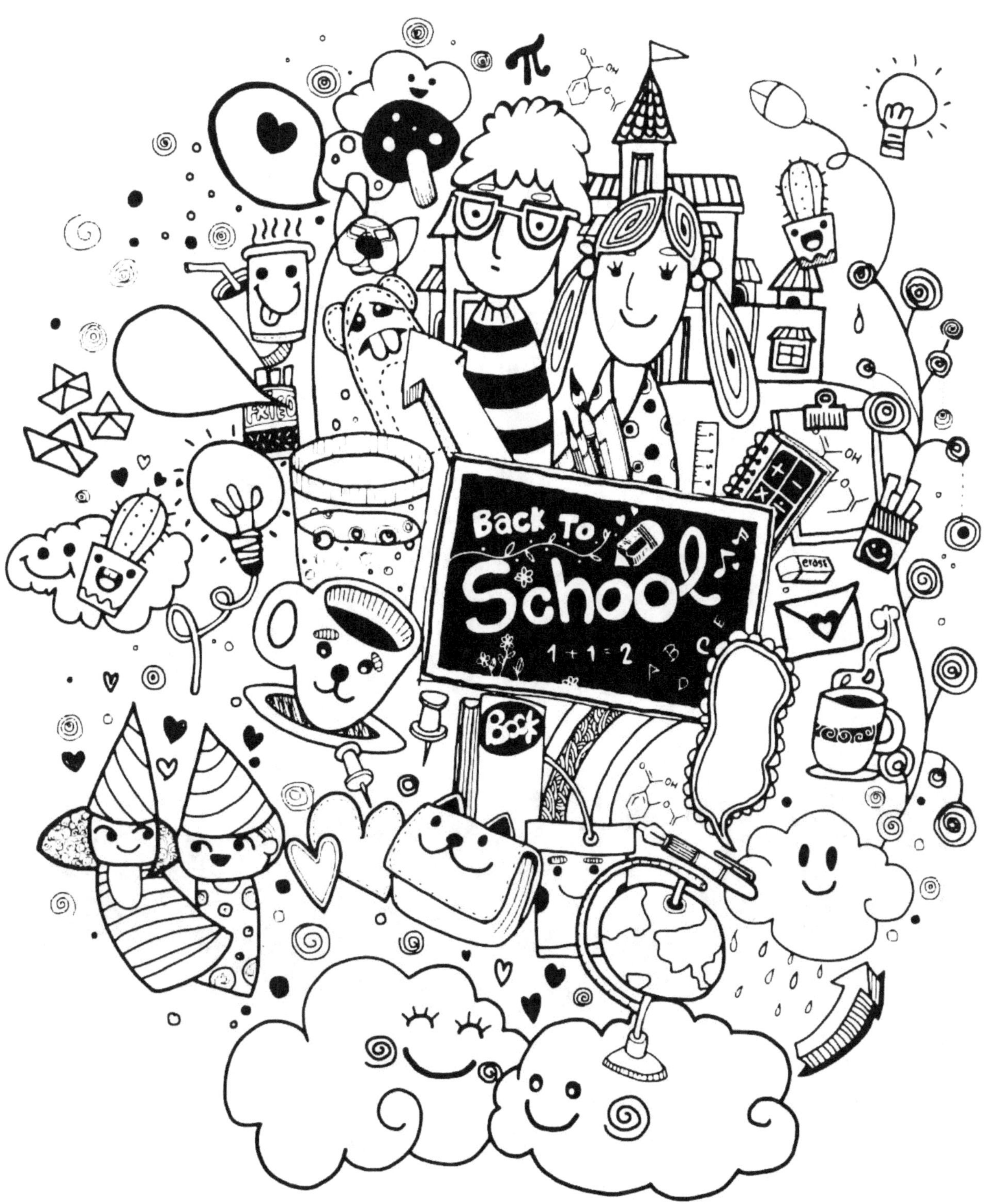

Back To
School
1 + 1 = 2 A B C
Book

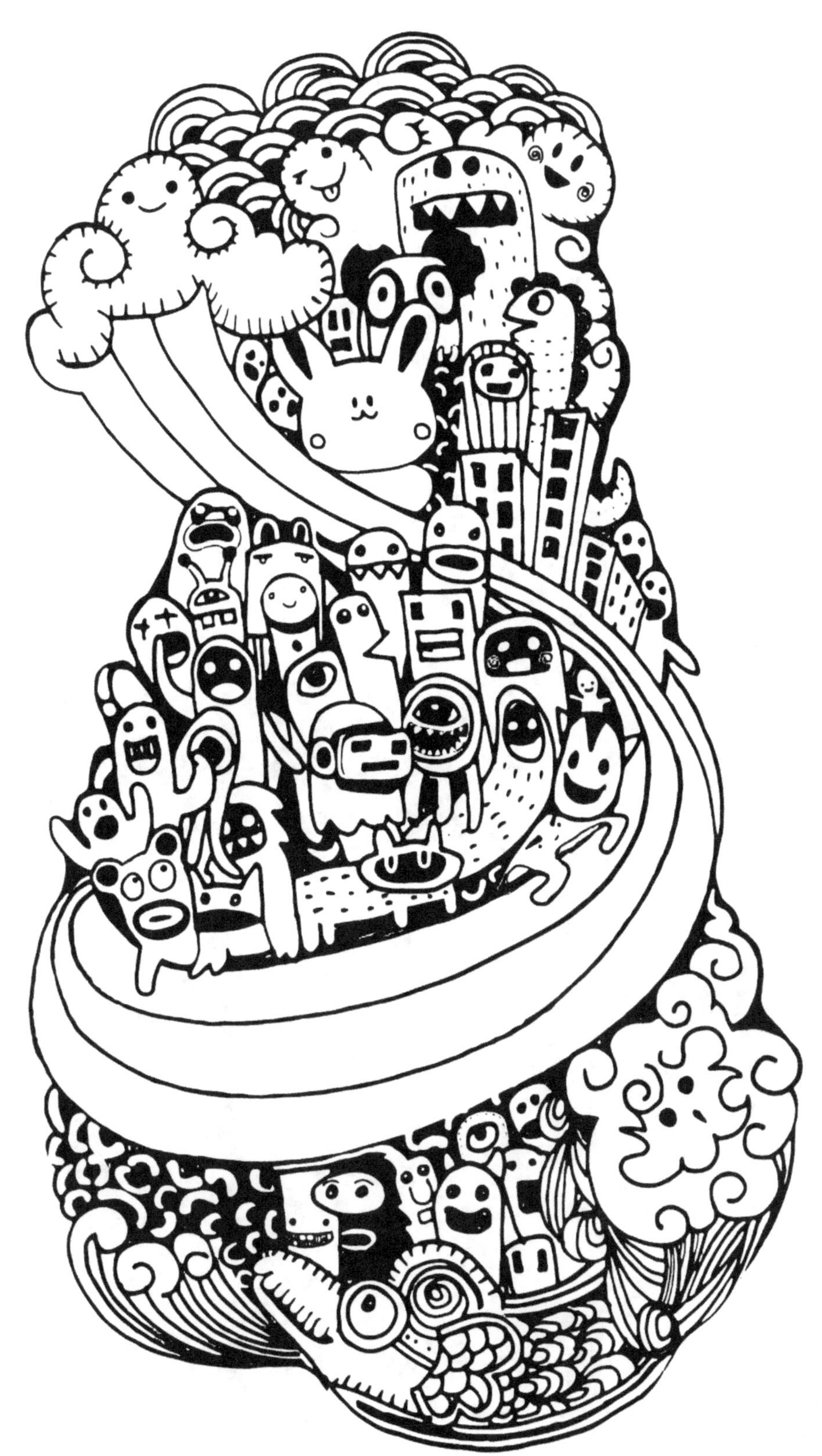

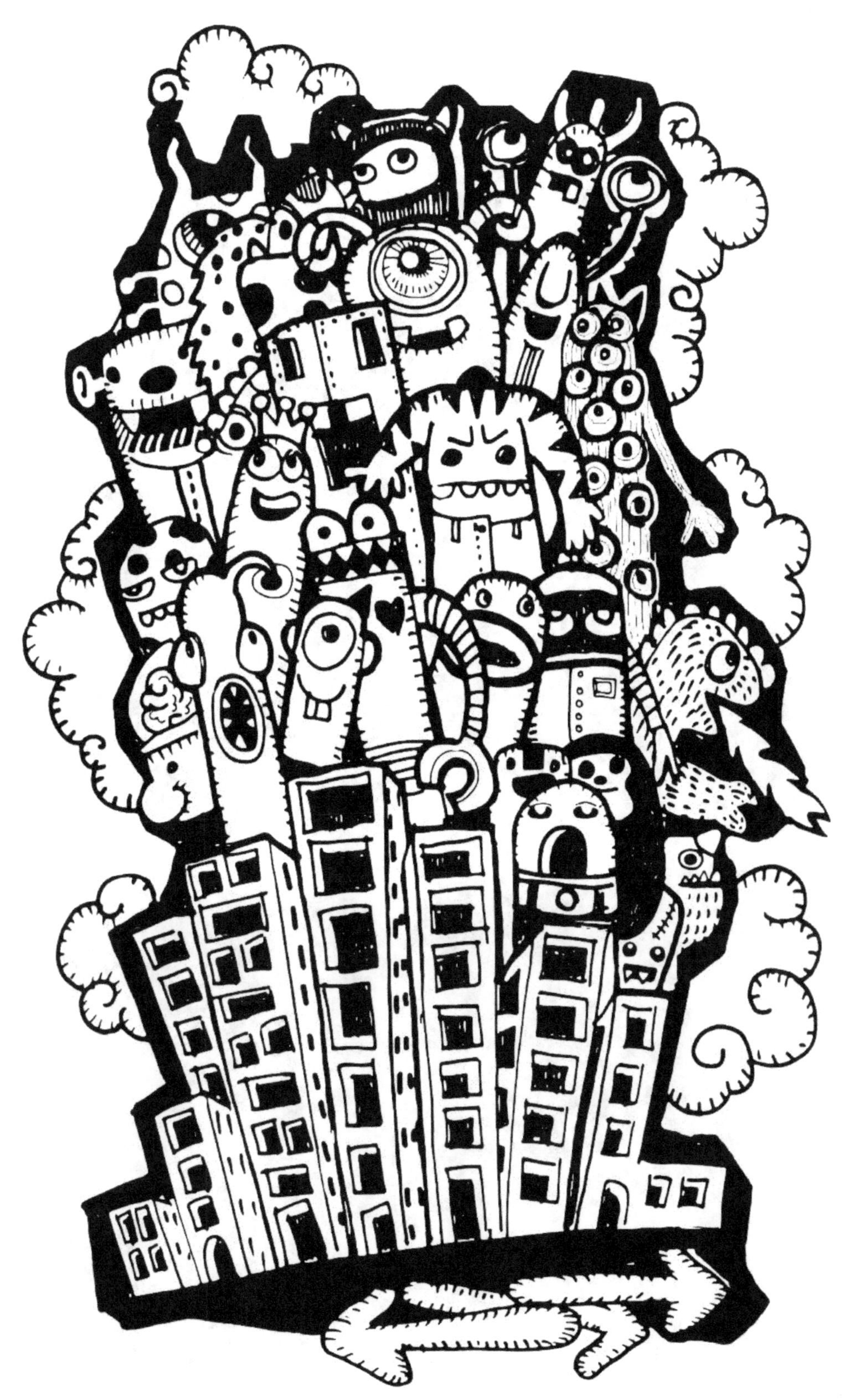

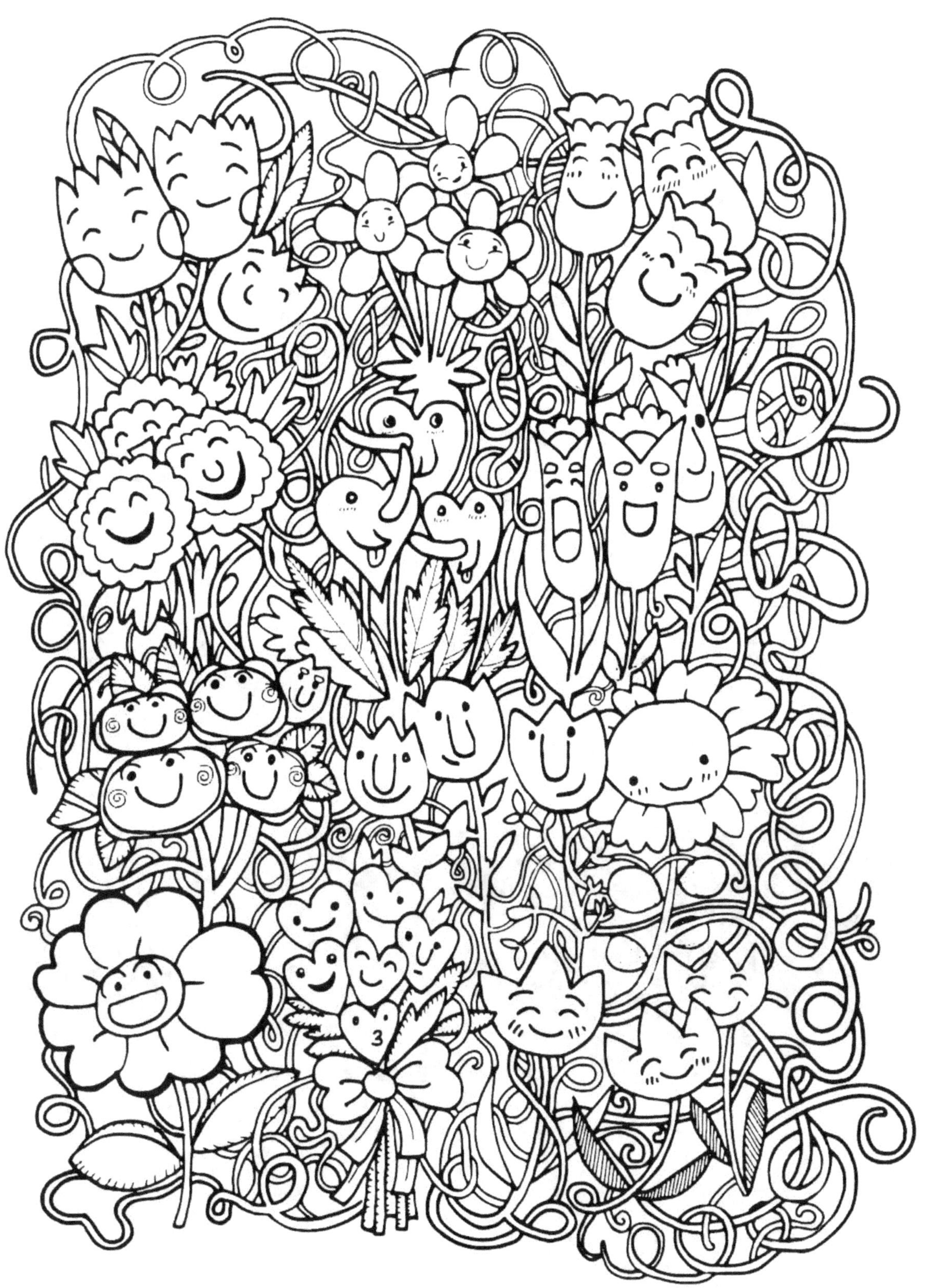

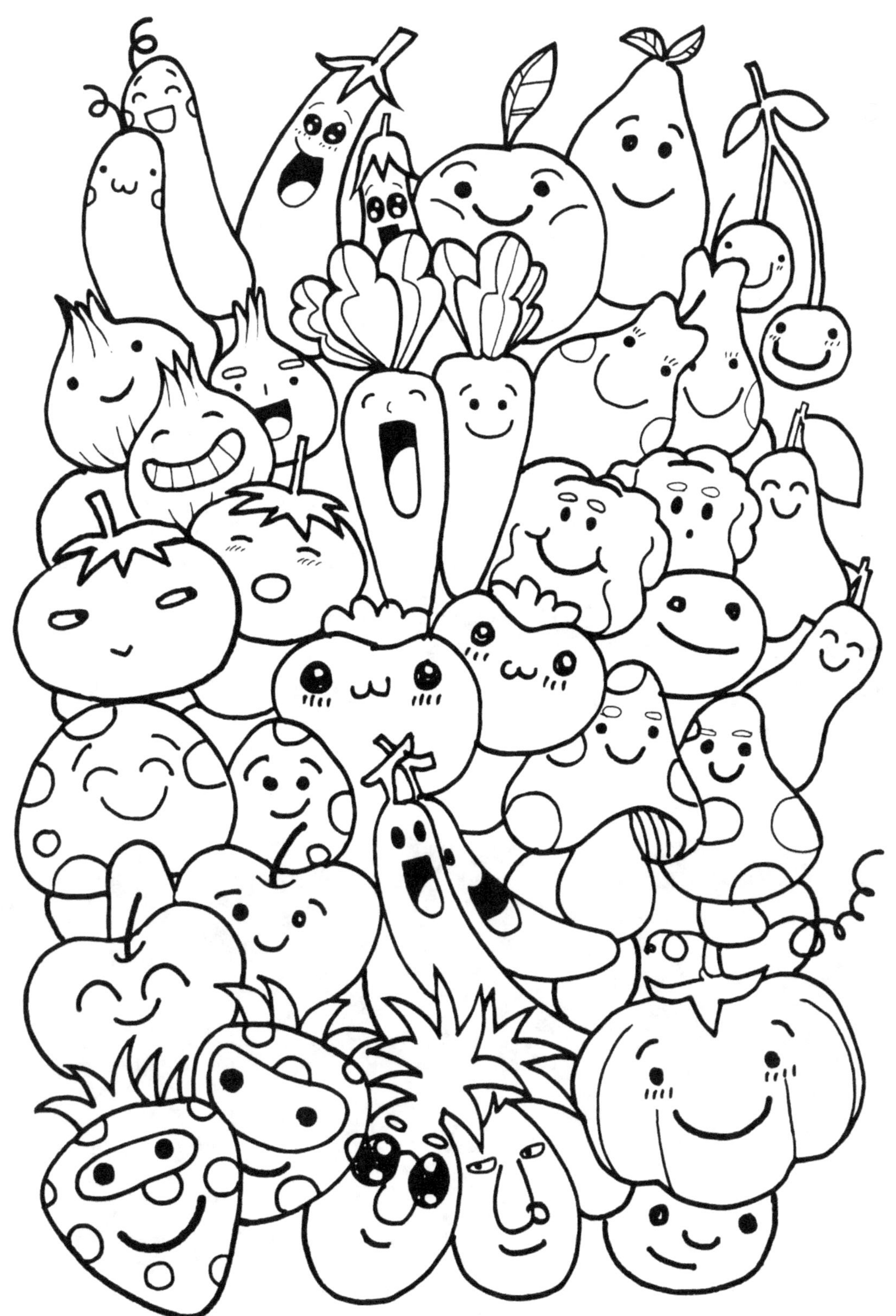

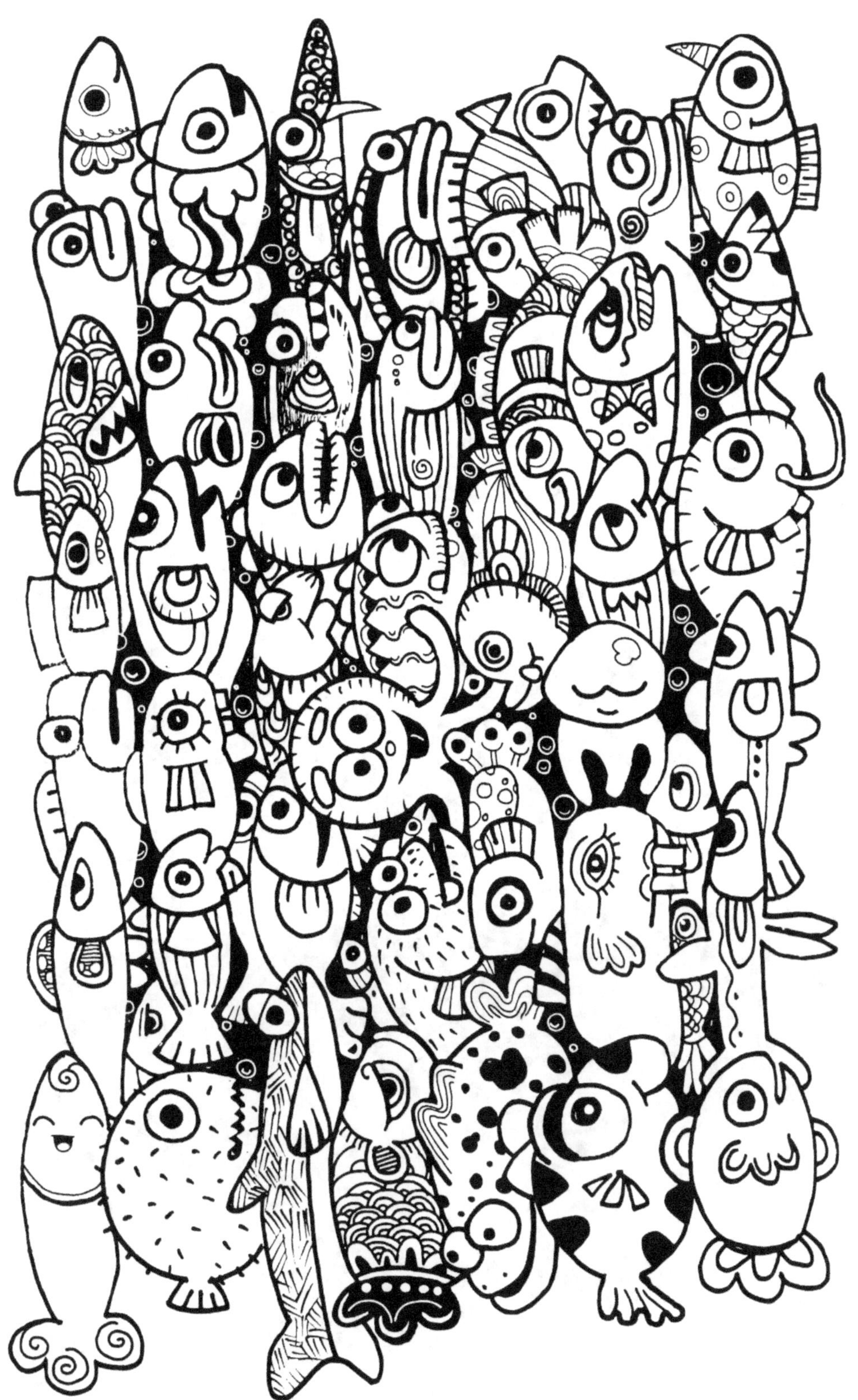

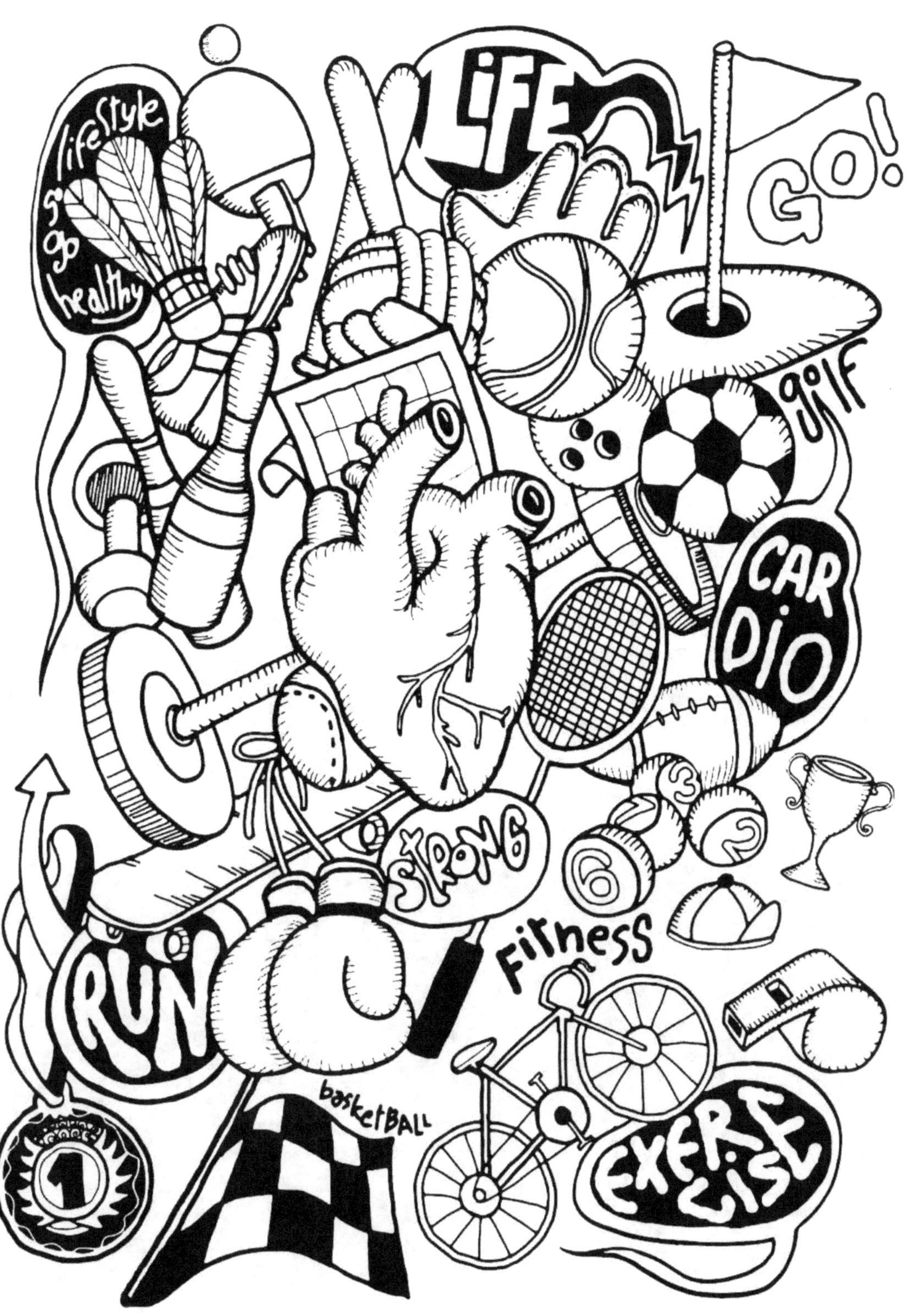

lifestyle go healthy
LIFE
GO!
golf
CARDIO
STRONG
3
2
6
fitness
RUN
basketBALL
1
EXERCISE

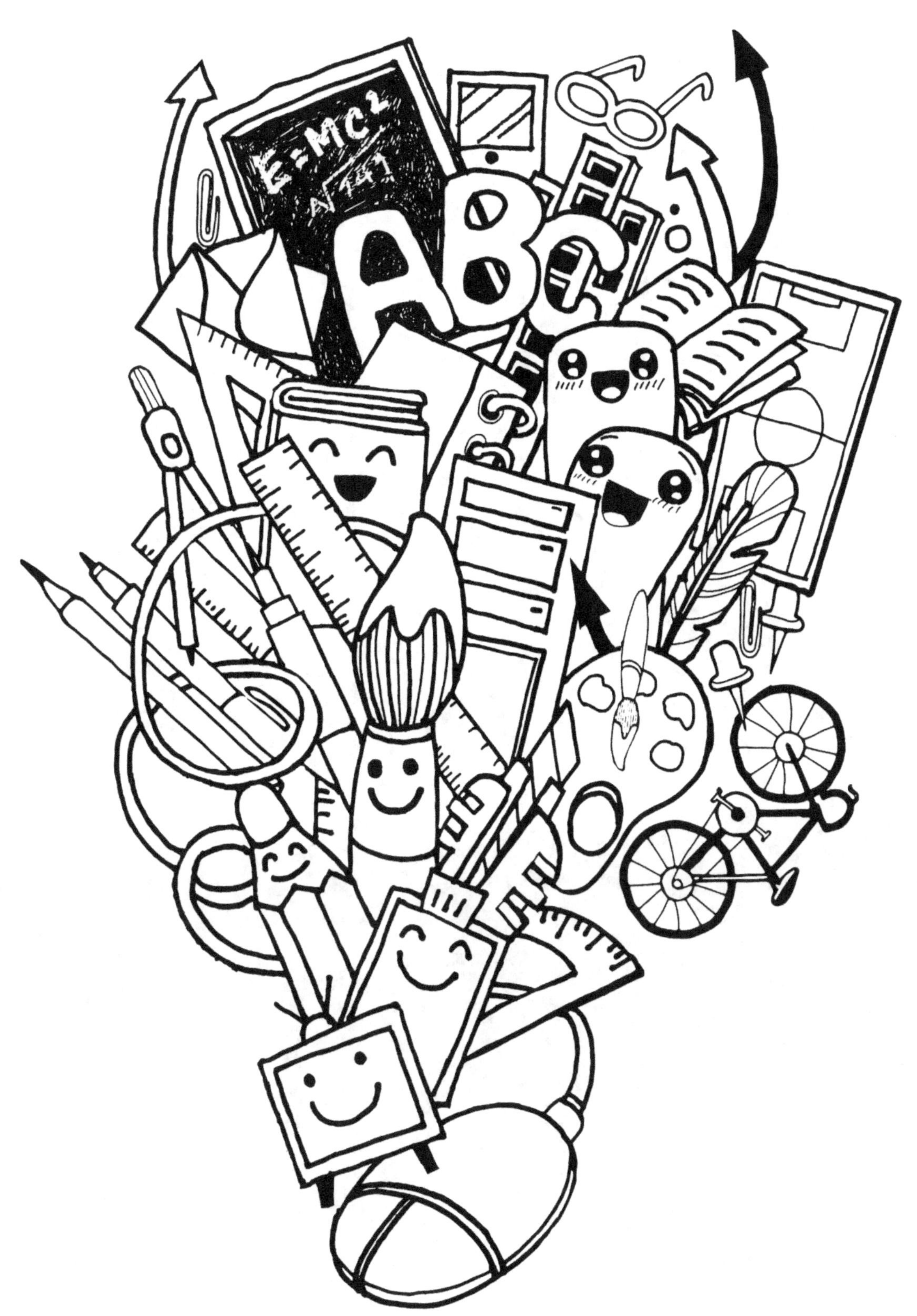

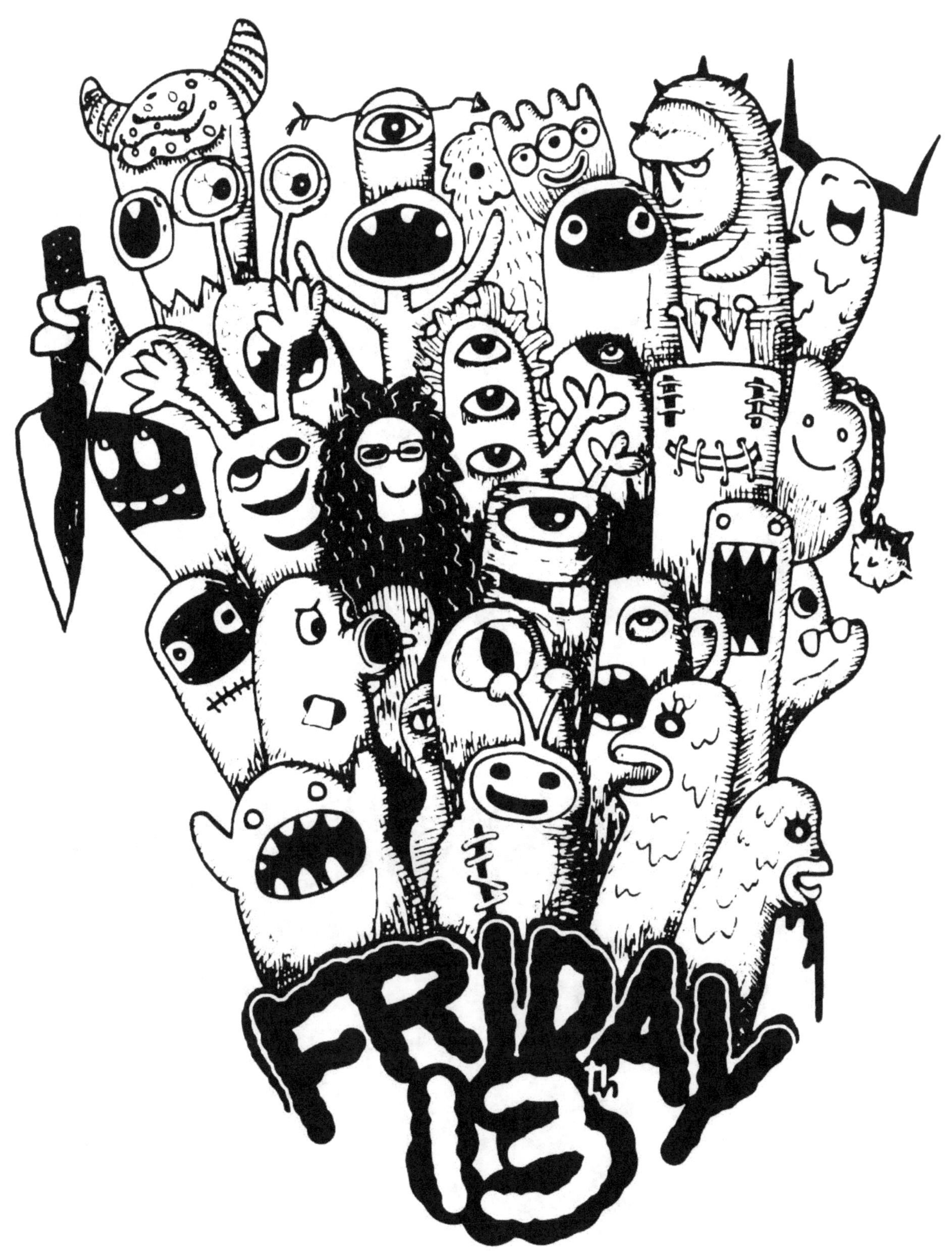

FRIDAY
13th

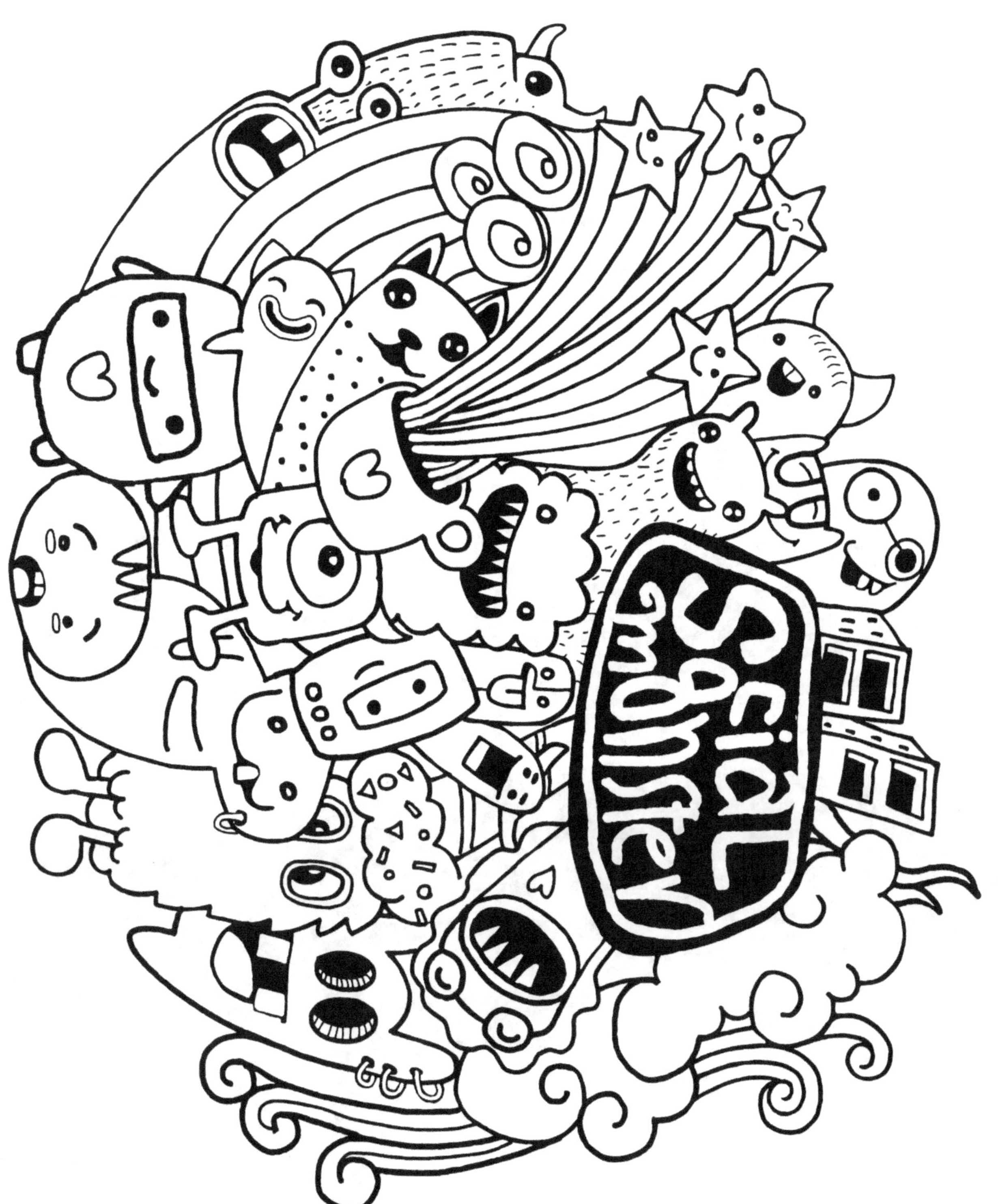

Social Monster

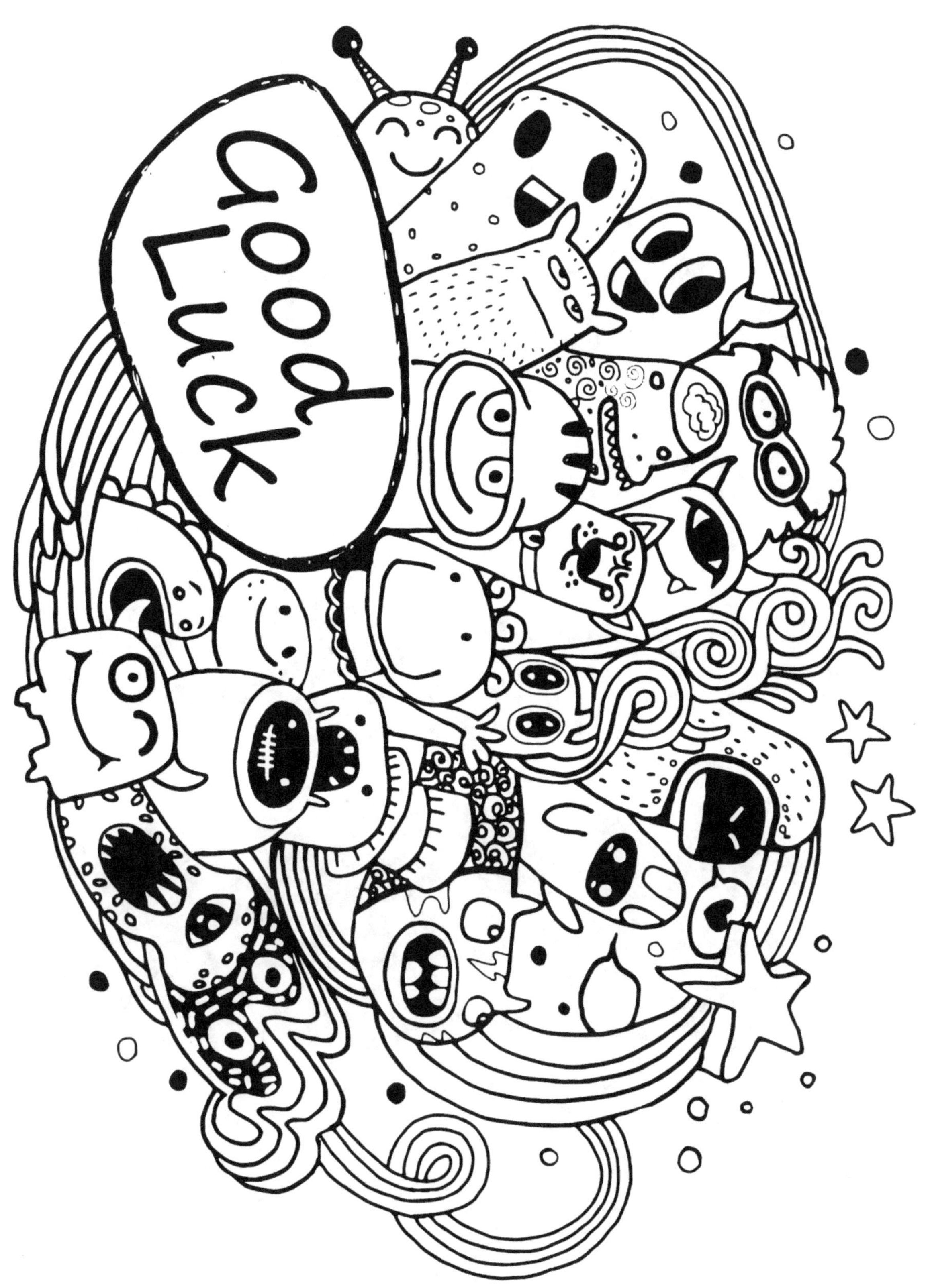

Good
Luck

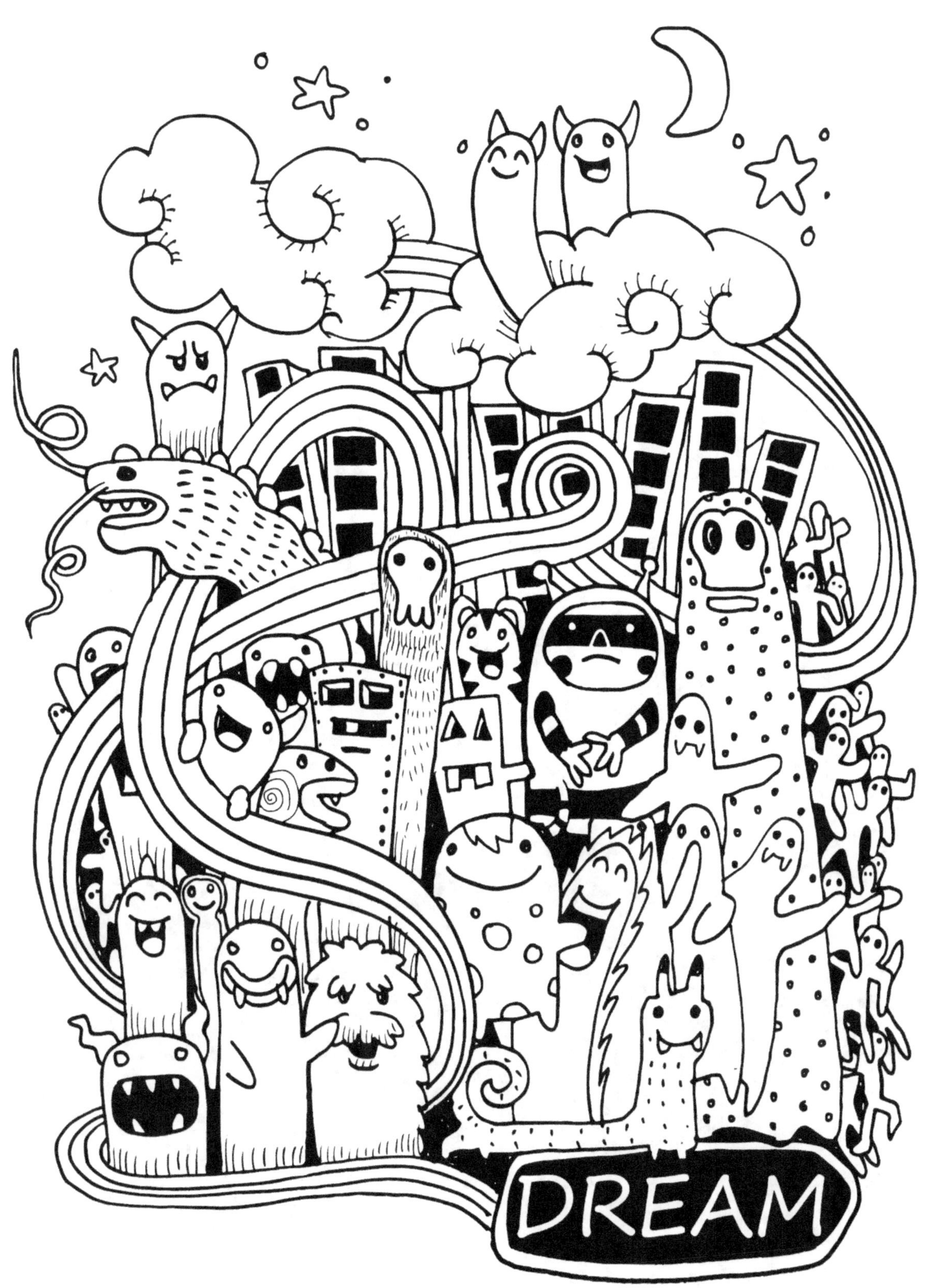

DREAM

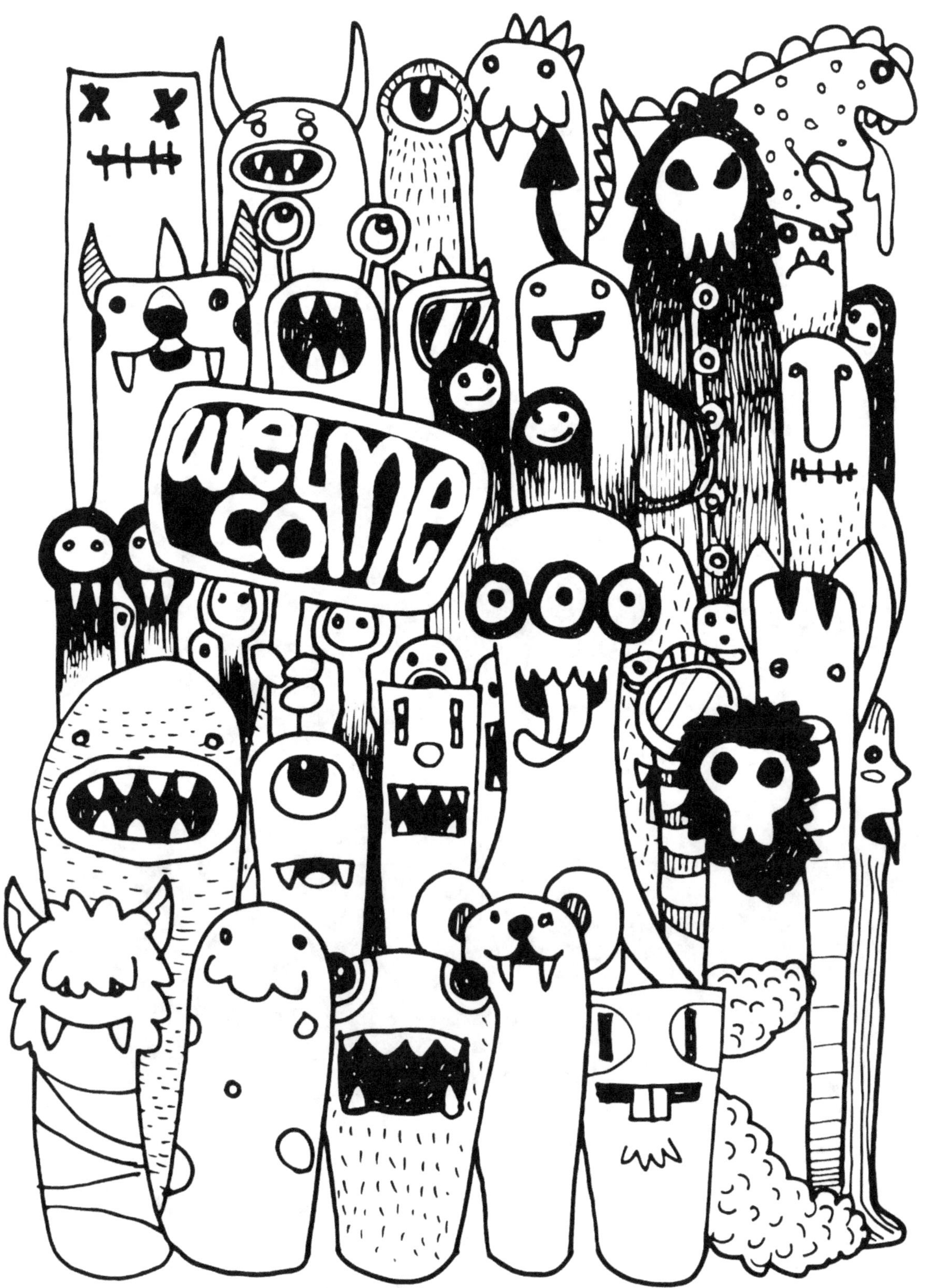

WEL
COME

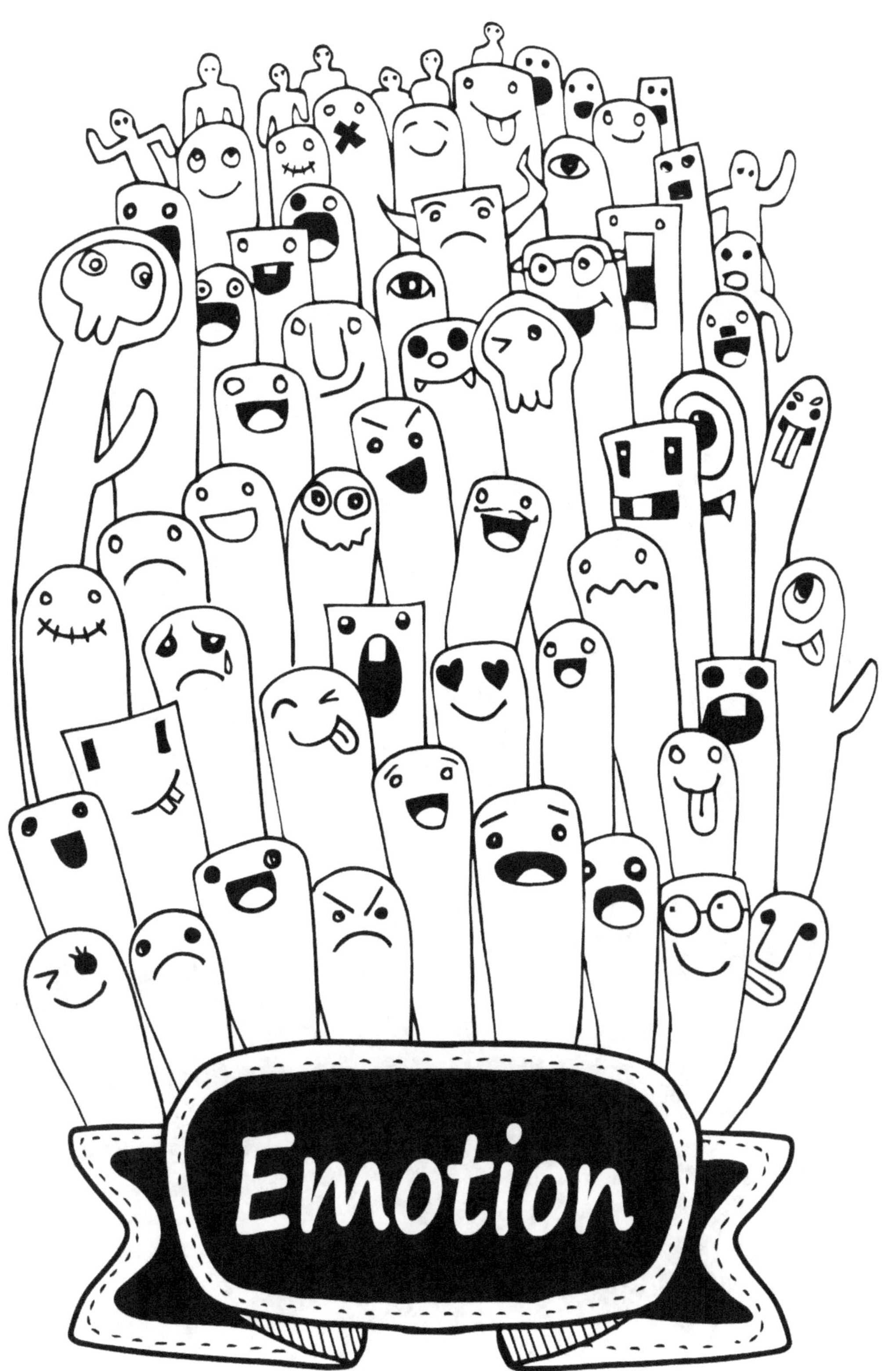
Emotion

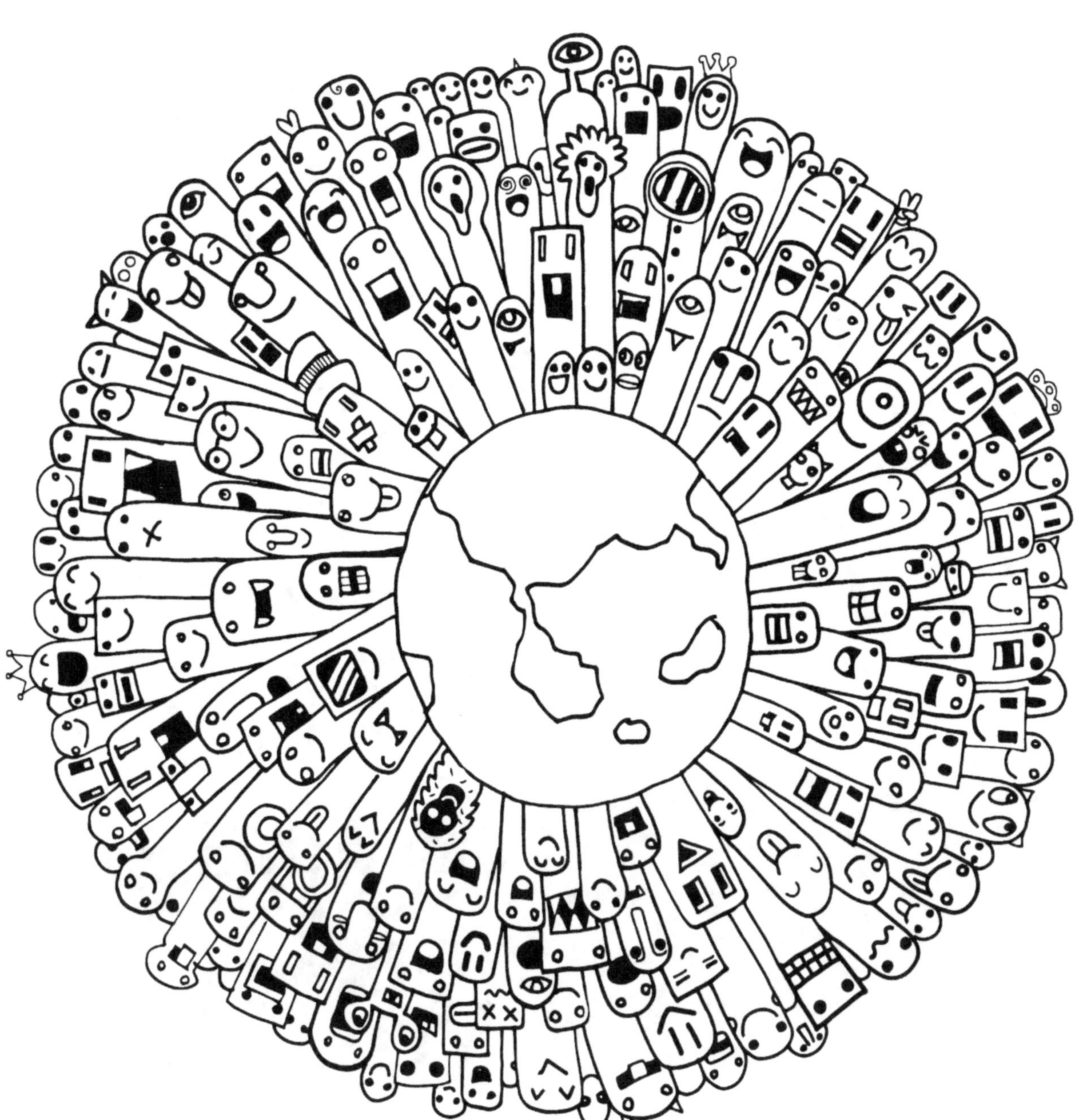

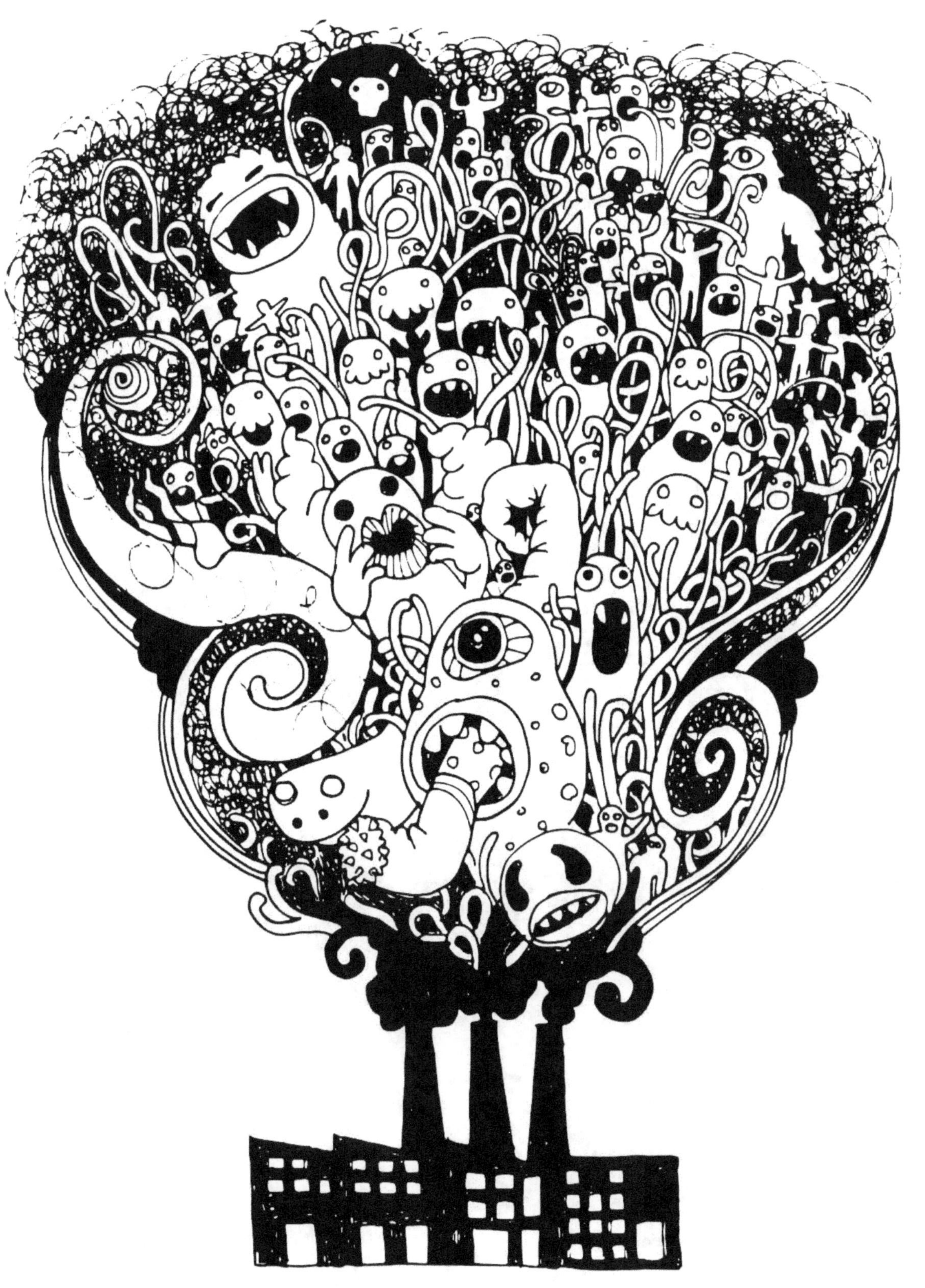

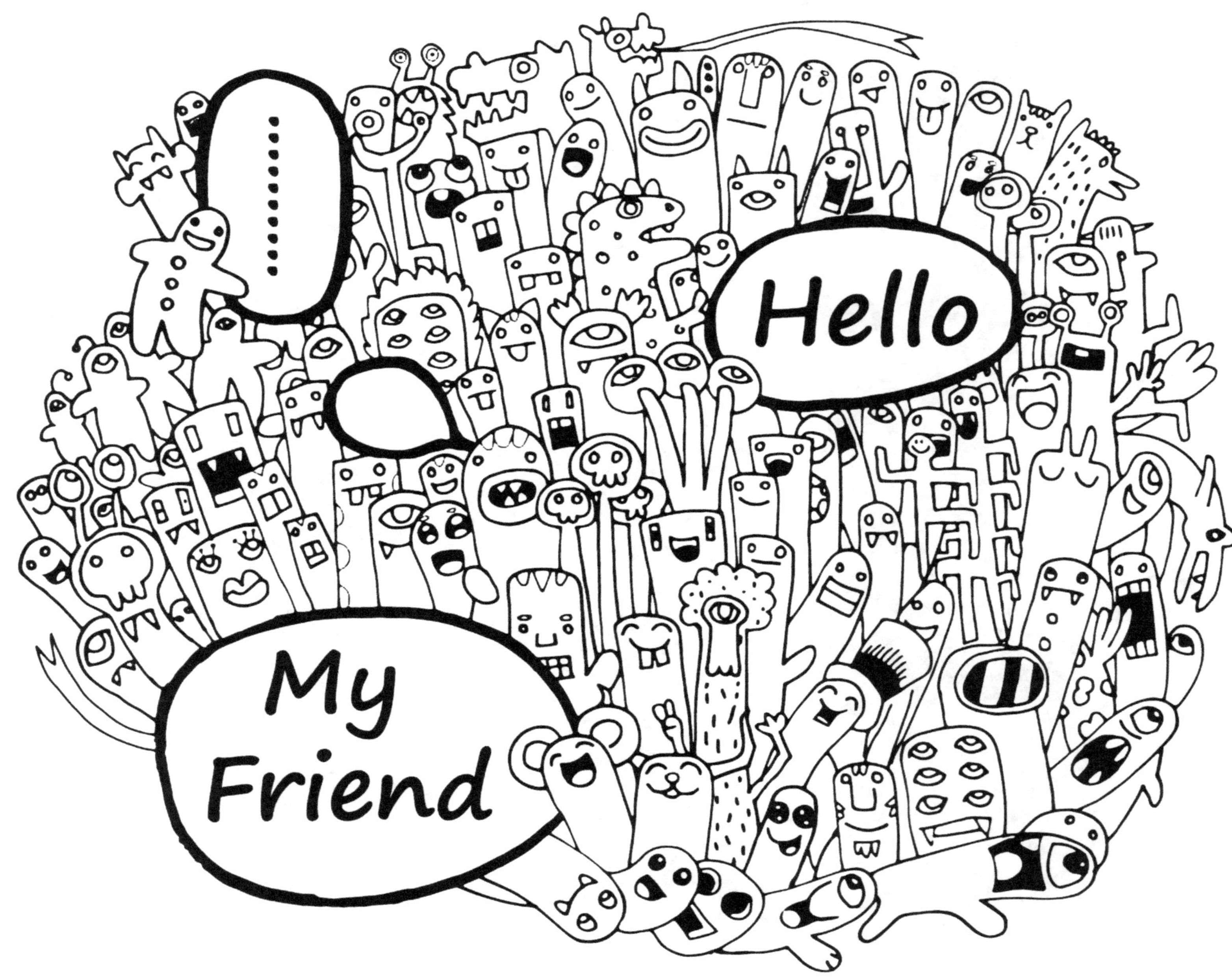

....
Hello
My Friend

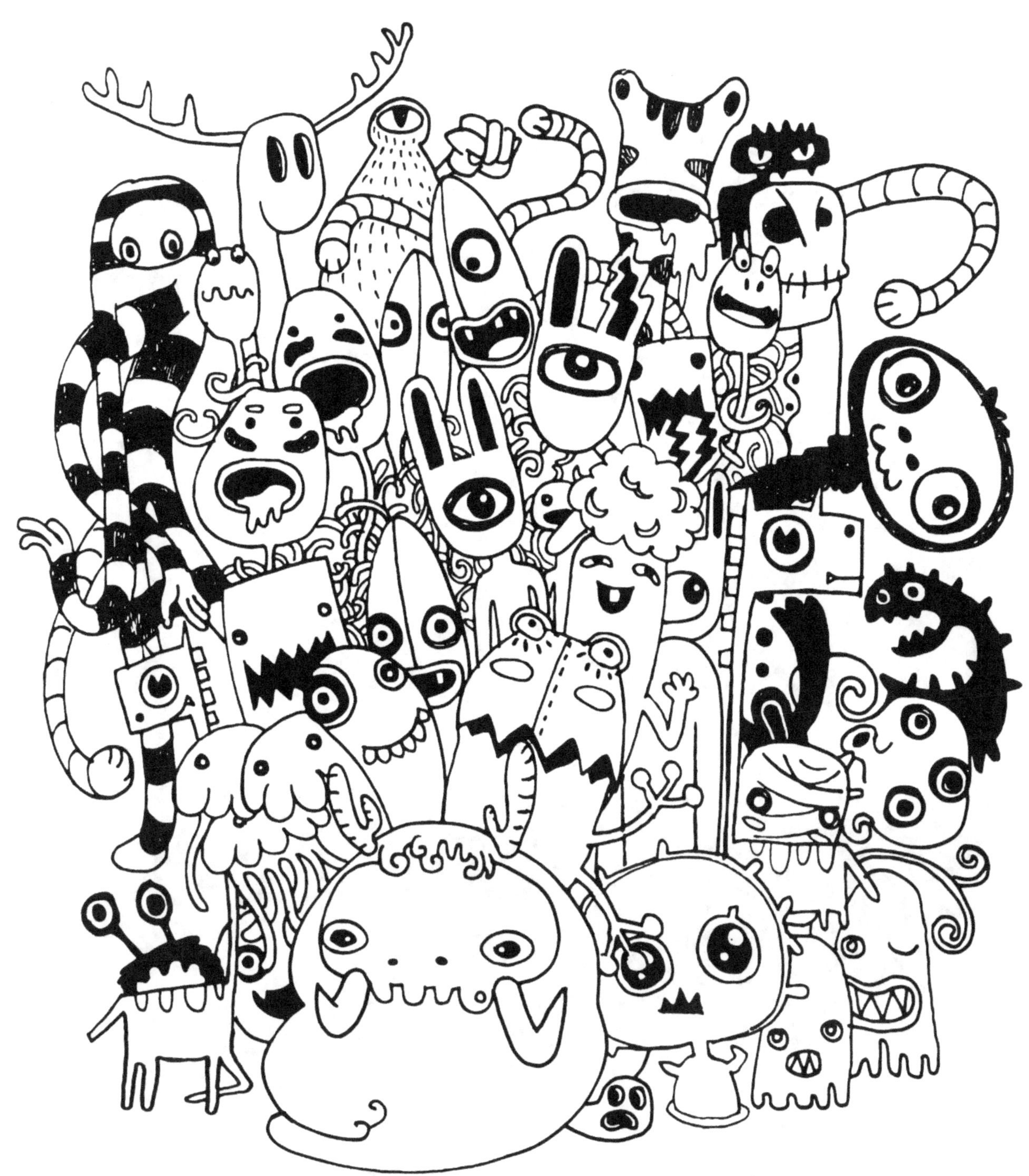

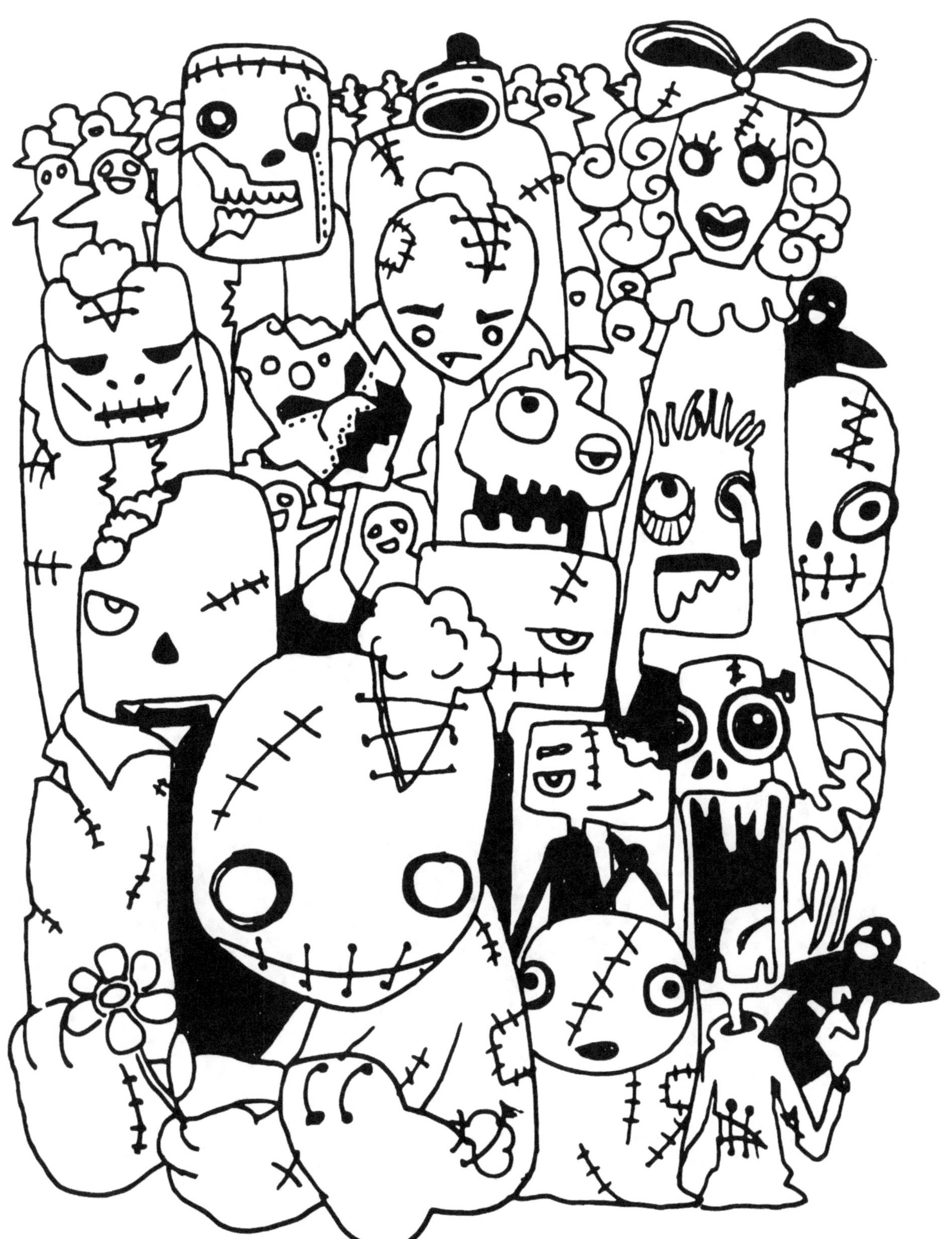

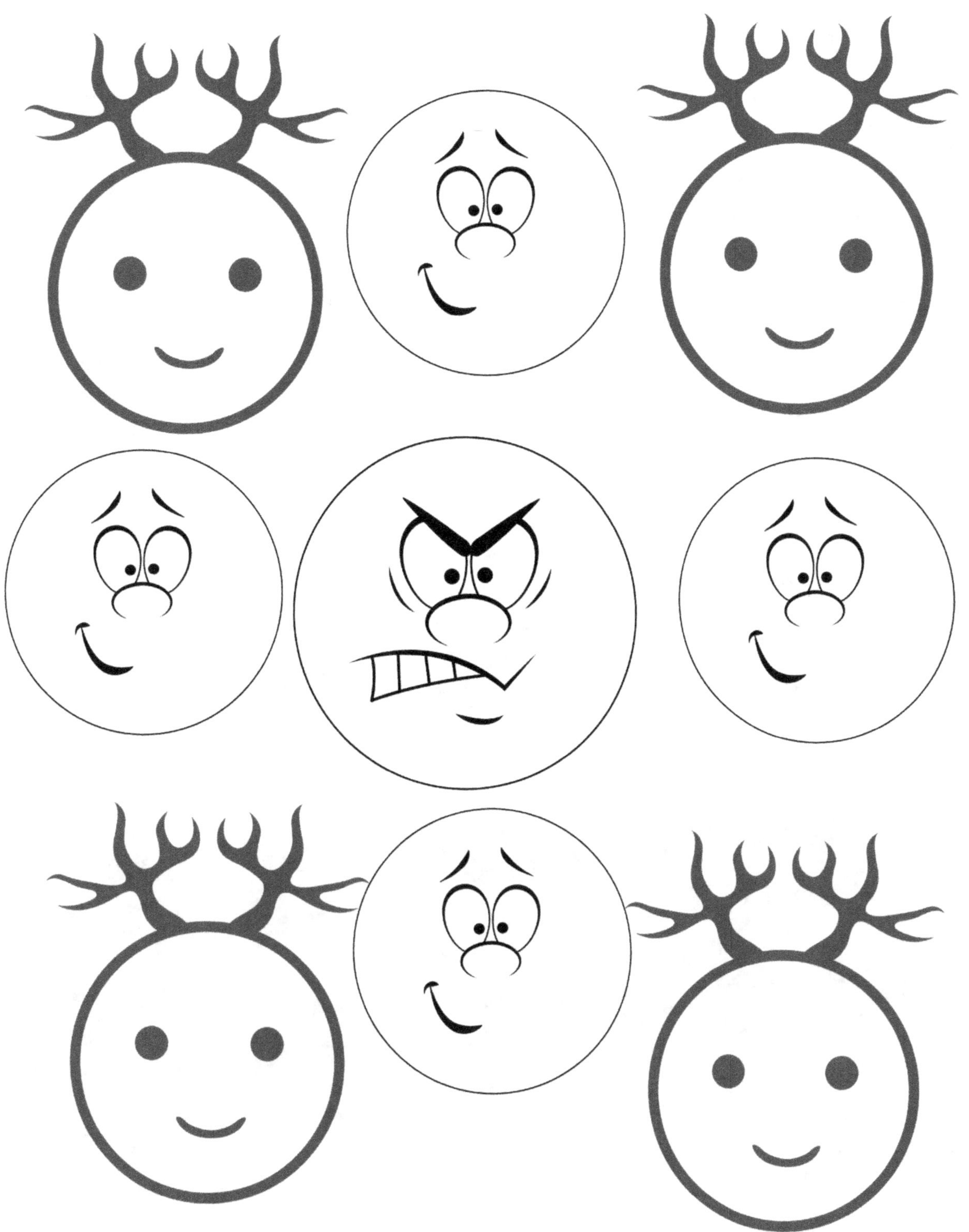

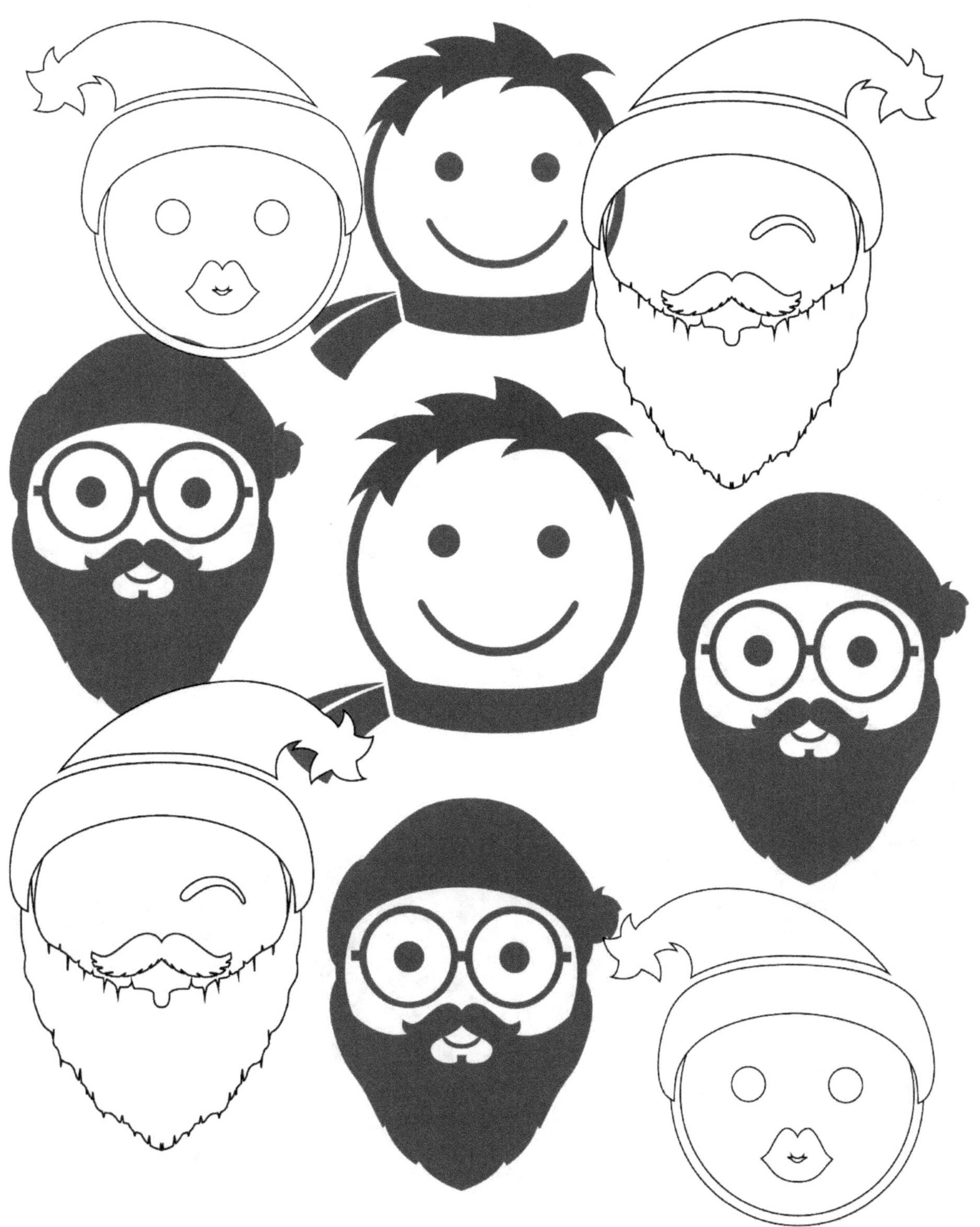

Thank You

Hope you've enjoyed your reading experience.
We here at Adriana P. Jenova will always strive to deliver to you the highest quality guides.
So I'd like to thank you for supporting us and reading until the very end.
Before you go, would you mind leaving us a review on Amazon?
It will mean a lot to us and support us creating high quality guides for you in the future.
Thanks once again and here's where you can leave a review.
Get Free Illustration Coloring Page Below
www.allcoloringbook.com

Warmly yours,
Adriana P. Jenova Team